Presidents

WILLIAM McKINLEY

A MyReportLinks.com Book

Stephen Feinstein

MyReportLinks.com Books
an imprint of
Enslow Publishers, Inc.
Box 398, 40 Industrial Road
Berkeley Heights, NJ 07922
USA

MyReportLinks.com Books, an imprint of Enslow Publishers, Inc.

Library of Congress Cataloging-in-Publication Data

Feinstein, Stephen.
　William McKinley: a MyReportLinks.com book / Stephen Feinstein.
　　p. cm. — (Presidents)
　Includes bibliographical references and index.
　ISBN 0-7660-5004-1
　1. McKinley, William, 1843–1901—Juvenile literature. 2. Presidents—United
States—Biography—Juvenile literature. [1. McKinley, William, 1843–1901. 2.
Presidents.] I. Title. II. Series.
　E711.6 .F46 2002
　973.8'8'092—dc21

　　　　　　　　　　　　　　　　　　　　　　　　　　　　　2001004302

Printed in the United States of America

10 9 8 7 6 5 4 3 2 1

To Our Readers: We have done our best to make sure all Internet addresses in this book
were active and appropriate when we went to press. However, the author and the Publisher
have no control over, and assume no liability for, the material available on those Internet
sites or on other Web sites they may link to. The Publisher will try to keep the Report Links
that back up this book up to date on our Web site for three years from the book's
first publication date. Any comments or suggestions can be sent by e-mail to
comments@myreportlinks.com or to the address on the back cover.

Photo Credits: © Corel Corporation, pp. 1 (background), 3; Courtesy of
American Memory, The Library of Congress, p. 42; Courtesy of Bartleby.com,
p. 29; Courtesy of MyReportLinks.com Books, p. 4; Courtesy of The American
President, pp. 14, 20, 22, 32; Courtesy of The Ohio State University Department
of History, pp. 24, 26, 35, 37; The Library of Congress, pp. 12, 19, 43; The
National Archives and Records Administration, pp. 31, 33, 39.

Cover Photo: © Corel Corporation; The Library of Congress.

Contents

About MyReportLinks.com Books

MyReportLinks.com Books
Great Books, Great Links, Great for Research!

MyReportLinks.com Books present the information you need to learn about your report subject. In addition, they show you where to go on the Internet for more information. The pre-evaluated Report Links, listed on **www.myreportlinks.com**, save hours of research time and link to dozens—even hundreds—of Web sites, source documents, and photos related to your report topic.

To Our Readers:

Each Report Link has been reviewed by our editors, who will work hard to keep only active and appropriate Internet addresses in our books and up to date on our Web site. However, the author and the Publisher have no control over, and assume no liability for, the material available on those Internet sites, or on other Web sites they may link to.

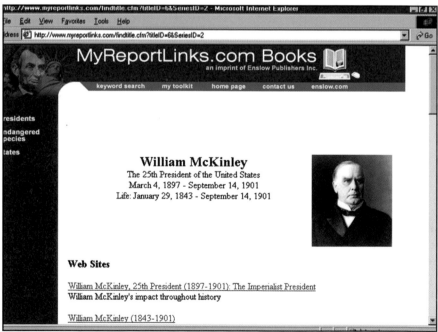

Access:

The Publisher will try to keep the Report Links that back up this book up to date on our Web site for three years from the book's first publication date. Please enter **PMC1563** if asked for a password.

Report Links

 The Internet sites described below can be accessed at
http://www.myreportlinks.com

*EDITOR'S CHOICE

▶ **William McKinley, 25th President (1897–1901):**
The Imperialist President

The American President series provides an extensive biography of
William McKinley. Learn how over the years historians have changed
their perception of McKinley and his administration.

Link to this Internet site from http://www.myreportlinks.com

*EDITOR'S CHOICE

▶ **William McKinley (1843–1901)**

This site provides a detailed biography of William McKinley. In
addition you will find links to information about McKinley's vice
president, cabinet members, related articles, study questions, and
additional resources.

Link to this Internet site from http://www.myreportlinks.com

*EDITOR'S CHOICE

▶ **The Era of William McKinley**

Created by Ohio State University's History Department, this site offers
a variety of insights into McKinley and the many offices he occupied.
One section features a look into the daily duties of President McKinley
as well as McKinley's relationship with the industrialist Mark Hanna.

Link to this Internet site from http://www.myreportlinks.com

*EDITOR'S CHOICE

▶ **McKinley Memorial Library & Museum**

This site provides an excellent introduction to the McKinley Memorial
Library and Museum, which is located in McKinley's birthplace of
Niles, Ohio.

Link to this Internet site from http://www.myreportlinks.com

*EDITOR'S CHOICE

▶ **William McKinley**

Part of the Internet Public Library's POTUS (Presidents of the United
States) series, this site provides a quick overview of William McKinley's
life and political career and links to an audio clip of McKinley's 1896
campaign speech from his front porch.

Link to this Internet site from http://www.myreportlinks.com

*EDITOR'S CHOICE

▶ **The American President, Episode 6:**
"The World Stage"

In The American President series, "The World Stage" profiles four
presidents who represented a nation during turbulent times. William
McKinley is one of the four featured.

Link to this Internet site from http://www.myreportlinks.com

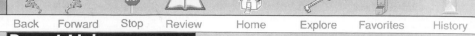
Report Links

The Internet sites described below can be accessed at
http://www.myreportlinks.com

▶**American Presidents: Life Portraits: William McKinley**
C-SPAN's American Presidents: Life Portraits series provides a quick
overview of McKinley's life and presidency. You can listen to a reading of a
letter written by President McKinley.

Link to this Internet site from http://www.myreportlinks.com

▶**The American Presidency: Ida Saxton McKinley**
This brief biography of Ida Saxton McKinley discusses the illness she suffered
for much of her adult life.

Link to this Internet site from http://www.myreportlinks.com

▶**The American Presidency: William McKinley**
Part of Grolier's The American Presidency series is a biography on William
McKinley. Grolier's assessment of McKinley's presidency credits McKinley
with significantly expanding presidential powers.

Link to this Internet site from http://www.myreportlinks.com

▶**America Votes: William McKinley—1896**
Featured in Duke University's America Votes Web site is a McKinley poster
from the election campaign of 1896. You will learn that James B. Duke was so
impressed by McKinley that he erected a statue of him on the grounds of his
New Jersey estate.

Link to this Internet site from http://www.myreportlinks.com

▶**The Atlantic Online: Mr. McKinley as President**
The Atlantic Online Web site presents an article about President McKinley
originally published in *The Atlantic Monthly* in March of 1901. In this article,
author Henry B.F. Macfarland discusses the McKinley administration and
dispels myths about McKinley's character.

Link to this Internet site from http://www.myreportlinks.com

▶**Hall of Presidents: William McKinley**
At this site you will find the portrait of William McKinley that hangs in the
Hall of Presidents in the National Portrait Gallery in Washington, D.C. The
oil on canvas painting was painted in 1897 by August Benziger.

Link to this Internet site from http://www.myreportlinks.com

Report Links

The Internet sites described below can be accessed at
http://www.myreportlinks.com

▶ **Infoplease.com: William McKinley**

Infoplease.com provides a brief biography of William McKinley,
which covers the highlights of his life.

Link to this Internet site from http://www.myreportlinks.com

▶ **The Last Days of a President: Films of McKinley and the
Pan-American Exposition, 1901**

This Library of Congress site contains twenty-eight films of McKinley
at the Pan-American Exposition. You will also read about America at
the turn of the century.

Link to this Internet site from http://www.myreportlinks.com

▶ **"Lights Out in the City of Light"—Images at the
Pan-American Exposition**

Part of the Libraries of the University of Buffalo Web site, this page
features photographs of William McKinley taken just before and
during his fateful trip to the Pan-American Exposition, in Buffalo.

Link to this Internet site from http://www.myreportlinks.com

▶ **Objects from the Presidency**

By navigating through this site you will find objects related to all
the United States presidents. You can also read a brief description
of McKinley, the era he lived in, and learn about the office of
the presidency.

Link to this Internet site from http://www.myreportlinks.com

▶ **The Ohio Historical Society: William McKinley**

Before becoming president, William McKinley served Ohio as a
congressman and governor. The Ohio Historical Society Web site's
review of McKinley's early life through his presidency reveals his
dedication to civil service.

Link to this Internet site from http://www.myreportlinks.com

▶ **President William McKinley**

This site provides an audio clip of William McKinley's "front-porch"
campaign speech from 1896. In addition you can read a comprehensive
account of McKinley's life and presidency.

Link to this Internet site from http://www.myreportlinks.com

Report Links

The Internet sites described below can be accessed at
http://www.myreportlinks.com

▶*Sunday Gazette-Mail* **Online: Czolgosz's crime changed the course of our nation**
The *Sunday Gazette-Mail* Online Web site contains an article written by Tom Searls titled "Czolgosz's crime changed the course of our nation." This article examines President McKinley's assassin, Leon Czolgosz.
Link to this Internet site from http://www.myreportlinks.com

▶**The White House: Ida Saxton McKinley**
In the official White House biography of Ida Saxton McKinley, you will learn how Ida Saxton met William McKinley while working as a cashier at her father's bank. Moreover, this biography discusses the illness that plagued her throughout her adult life and how her husband coped with it.
Link to this Internet site from http://www.myreportlinks.com

▶**The White House: William McKinley**
At this White House site, you will learn that under President William McKinley, the United States acquired its first overseas possessions. This profile of the twenty-fifth president provides an excellent overview of his life before the presidency.
Link to this Internet site from http://www.myreportlinks.com

▶**William McKinley**
Lycos Zone's Fact Monster is an exciting site where you will find lots of interesting information, including a biography of William McKinley. You will be introduced to many of the key events in McKinley's life before and during his presidency.
Link to this Internet site from http://www.myreportlinks.com

▶**William McKinley**
Interlink Cafe provides a number of presidential speeches, including McKinley's inaugural addresses, his Annual Messages to Congress, and his 1898 War Message. This site also provides a number of links to other McKinley sites.
Link to this Internet site from http://www.myreportlinks.com

▶**William McKinley: First Inaugural Address**
Bartleby.com provides a vast electronic library wherein you will find McKinley's First Inaugural Address. Delivered on March 4, 1897, McKinley pledged to revive the nation's economy after four years of an economic depression.
Link to this Internet site from http://www.myreportlinks.com

Report Links

  The Internet sites described below can be accessed at
http://www.myreportlinks.com

▶ **William McKinley: Second Inaugural Address**
On March 4, 1901, McKinley delivered his Second Inaugural Address.
Read about the patriotic celebration that followed the ending of the
Spanish-American War.

Link to this Internet site from http://www.myreportlinks.com

▶ **William McKinley: Who Was Bill McKinley?**
ThinkQuest presents a biography of William McKinley. By navigating
through the various links on this site you will learn about the Spanish-
American War and how the United States acquired territory for
colonization for the first time.

Link to this Internet site from http://www.myreportlinks.com

▶ **William McKinley (1843–1901)**
The Spanish-American War Centennial Web site contains a wealth of
information including McKinley's 1898 Declaration of War letter and a
detailed account of the destruction of the USS *Maine*.

Link to this Internet site from http://www.myreportlinks.com

▶ **William McKinley, 25th President (1897–1901)**
This profile of President McKinley explores the relationship between
McKinley and Mark Hanna. You will learn that despite newspaper
characterizations of McKinley's relationship with Hanna, McKinley
remained his own man.

Link to this Internet site from http://www.myreportlinks.com

▶ **The World of 1898: The Spanish-American War**
The Spanish-American War was one of the most significant events in
McKinley's presidency. The Library of Congress provides an excellent
introduction to the events that led up to the war and McKinley's
involvement.

Link to this Internet site from http://www.myreportlinks.com

▶ **1896: William McKinley vs. William Jennings Bryan**
This site provides a summary of the election of 1896. You will also find
other links related to the election.

Link to this Internet site from http://www.myreportlinks.com

Highlights

1843—*Jan. 29:* Born in Niles, Ohio.

1861–1865—Serves with Twenty-third Ohio Volunteer Infantry. Reaches rank of brevet major.

1867—Admitted to Ohio Bar Association, that state's association of lawyers.

1869—Elected county prosecutor for Clark County, Ohio.

1871—*Jan. 25:* Marries Ida Saxton in Canton, Ohio.

1876—Elected to the House of Representatives.

1891—Elected governor of Ohio.

1896—Elected twenty-fifth president of the United States, defeating William Jennings Bryan.

1898—Signs congressional resolution annexing the Hawaiian Islands. Asks for declaration of war against Spain in what came to be known as the Spanish-American War. In the Paris Peace Treaty, the United States receives Cuba, Puerto Rico, Guam, and the Philippine Islands in exchange for 20 million dollars.

1899—Asks Secretary of State John Hay to issue Open Door policy toward China.

1900—Reelected president, again defeating William Jennings Bryan.

1901—*Sep. 6:* Shot by Leon F. Czolgosz, a self-proclaimed anarchist.

Sep. 14: Dies in Buffalo, New York, from complications due to the gunshot wounds.

Oct. 29: Czolgosz is put to death by electric chair at Auburn State Prison in New York.

"Don't Let Them Hurt Him"

William McKinley, America's twenty-fifth president, should have listened to the advice of his personal secretary, George Cortelyou. If he had, the national tragedy that occurred on September 6, 1901, could have been averted.

The day before, President McKinley had given a speech at the Pan-American Exposition in Buffalo, New York. Fifty thousand listeners responded enthusiastically as McKinley portrayed America as a world power. The next day, McKinley planned to greet his admirers with a presidential handshake. Cortelyou, concerned for the president's safety, did not approve of the plan.

When Cortelyou advised McKinley to cancel the public reception, McKinley refused, seeing no cause for concern. After all, McKinley was greatly admired and loved by the public. Even his political opponents liked and respected him because of his warm and friendly personality. So plans for the reception were finalized, and a public announcement was made. On September 6, there would be a ten-minute reception at 4:00 P.M. at the Temple of Music on the fairgrounds of the Pan-American Exposition.

That morning, McKinley, his wife, and a group of close associates and distinguished guests visited nearby Niagara Falls. The day's activities had been scheduled to provide relaxation and pleasure. The president and his party returned to the fairgrounds in the afternoon. Thus far, McKinley was thoroughly enjoying the day, and he was looking forward to the brief public reception.

At four o'clock, McKinley was at the Temple of Music, preparing to greet the public. The doors opened, and people filed in. Excitement filled the air as, one by one, the people approached their president. McKinley smiled at each person as he shook hands with each. Because it was a very warm day, handkerchiefs appeared around the hall as people mopped their brows. Perhaps that is why nobody, including the president's Secret Service agents, noticed the young man with a handkerchief wrapped around his right hand.

The man with the handkerchief, twenty-eight-year-old Leon Czolgosz, stepped up to McKinley, who reached out to shake his hand. Hidden beneath the handkerchief was a gun. Suddenly two shots rang out as Czolgosz fired his

▲ The assassination of President William McKinley at the Pan-American Exposition on September 6, 1901, is depicted in this painting. Leon Czolgosz shot the president with a revolver that was concealed by a handkerchief.

revolver at McKinley. The president stared at the young man in disbelief before collapsing into the arms of a Secret Service agent. People in the crowd grabbed the gunman and began beating him, as McKinley was helped into a chair. Hysterical screaming rocked the room. Although bleeding and in shock, McKinley, admired by many for his kindness, called out, "Don't let them hurt him."[1] And then, to a devastated Cortelyou, who leaned over him, he whispered, "My wife—be careful, Cortelyou, how you tell her—oh, be careful."[2]

While being treated for his wounds, McKinley seemed to express sympathy for Czolgosz, assuming the poor man was somehow misguided. Czolgosz claimed to be an anarchist who hated the government. He said he had shot President McKinley because, "I didn't believe one man should have so much service and another man should have none."[3]

Although it was not apparent at first, the president had been mortally wounded. One of the bullets had hit a button and only bruised McKinley, but the other bullet entered his abdomen. Surgeons treating the president cleaned and closed the wounds, but were unable to find and remove the bullet. McKinley died on September 14, 1901. The nation mourned the loss of its twenty-fifth president, who died just six months into his second term of office.

Chapter 2

Early Years, 1843–1861

William McKinley, Jr., was born on January 29, 1843, at the family home in the little country town of Niles, Ohio. He was the seventh of eight children born to William and Nancy Allison McKinley (a ninth child died in infancy). William, Jr., had four sisters and three brothers.

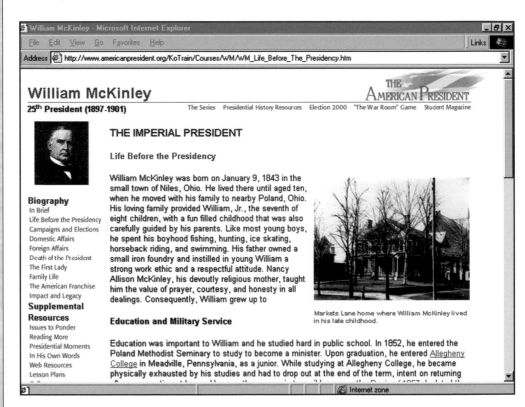

William McKinley - Microsoft Internet Explorer

File   Edit   View   Go   Favorites   Help   Links

Address http://www.americanpresident.org/KoTrain/Courses/WM/WM_Life_Before_The_Presidency.htm

William McKinley
25th President (1897-1901)

THE AMERICAN PRESIDENT

The Series   Presidential History Resources   Election 2000   "The War Room" Game   Student Magazine

THE IMPERIAL PRESIDENT

Life Before the Presidency

Biography
In Brief
Life Before the Presidency
Campaigns and Elections
Domestic Affairs
Foreign Affairs
Death of the President
The First Lady
Family Life
The American Franchise
Impact and Legacy
Supplemental Resources
Issues to Ponder
Reading More
Presidential Moments
In His Own Words
Web Resources
Lesson Plans

William McKinley was born on January 9, 1843 in the small town of Niles, Ohio. He lived there until aged ten, when he moved with his family to nearby Poland, Ohio. His loving family provided William, Jr., the seventh of eight children, with a fun filled childhood that was also carefully guided by his parents. Like most young boys, he spent his boyhood fishing, hunting, ice skating, horseback riding, and swimming. His father owned a small iron foundry and instilled in young William a strong work ethic and a respectful attitude. Nancy Allison McKinley, his devoutly religious mother, taught him the value of prayer, courtesy, and honesty in all dealings. Consequently, William grew up to

Markets Lane home where William McKinley lived in his late childhood.

Education and Military Service

Education was important to William and he studied hard in public school. In 1852, he entered the Poland Methodist Seminary to study to become a minister. Upon graduation, he entered Allegheny College in Meadville, Pennsylvania, as a junior. While studying at Allegheny College, he became physically exhausted by his studies and had to drop out at the end of the term, intent on returning

Internet zone

▲ William McKinley was born in the small town of Niles, Ohio, where he lived until the age of ten. His family then moved to nearby Poland, Ohio.

Young William, Jr.

The McKinleys were devout Methodists of Scots-Irish heritage. William, Jr., was a serious and gentle child who enjoyed the company of his mother and sisters and was greatly influenced by his mother's religious devotion. Although William was a serious young boy, he loved to play as much as other boys his age. At the time of the Mexican War, he and his playmates pretended to be soldiers. They paraded around wearing paper hats and carrying wooden swords. Besides playing, young William was expected to perform various chores around the house, as well as driving the family's cows to and from pasture.

A Serious Student

As a child, William had a curious nature and seemed to be interested in everything. He learned the basic subjects—reading, writing, and arithmetic—at Alva Sanford's one-room school-house, the public school in Niles. In 1852, the McKinleys moved ten miles away to the larger town of Poland, Ohio. Poland offered better schools than Niles. William briefly attended public school in Poland but soon enrolled in the Poland Seminary, a Methodist institution.

At the Poland Seminary, nine-year-old William became totally absorbed in his studies and was rarely seen without a book in his hands. At the seminary he discovered that he had a talent for public speaking, and speech became William's favorite subject. He enjoyed debating other students in a wide range of subjects including philosophy, history, and literature.

In 1860, at age seventeen, William entered Allegheny College, in Meadville, Pennsylvania, as a junior. There, the serious student threw himself into his studies with

total devotion. Still, trouble loomed ahead. Within a few months, he became physically exhausted and ill. He was forced to drop out of college.

An Unfortunate Setback

McKinley returned home to Poland, determined to return to school once he had regained his health. This did not happen right away. During the economic depression following the Panic of 1857, McKinley's family suffered a financial setback. Now there was no money for McKinley's education. William would have to go to work to help support his family.

The Kerr District School in Poland needed to fill a vacant teaching position. McKinley applied for the job and was hired. Every day, McKinley walked the three miles from his family's home to the school. At the end of the day he walked back home again. McKinley earned twenty-five dollars a month during the school session. When the term was over in the spring of 1861, McKinley found a job as a clerk in the Poland post office. He planned to return to college in Pennsylvania as soon as he had saved up enough money.

Most likely, McKinley would have resumed his college education that year. But something happened in April that caused a change in his plans: the Civil War began. McKinley, like hundreds of thousands of other young American men, would soon find himself caught up in the war.

Chapter 3 ▶

Civil War Soldier to Lawyer, 1861–1867

For many years, relations between the northern and southern states had been growing increasingly tense, principally over the issue of slavery. The situation reached a boiling point when Abraham Lincoln was elected to the presidency in 1860. Southerners were afraid that Lincoln would act to abolish slavery, thereby destroying the economy of the South and the slave owners' traditional way of life. Eleven southern states seceded from the Union and formed the Confederate States of America.

▶ The Civil War

The Civil War began on April 21, 1861, when Confederate forces attacked and seized Fort Sumter, the Union garrison at Charleston, South Carolina. Throughout the North, volunteers flocked to enlist in the Union army. In Poland, Ohio, a town meeting was held in June 1861. Eighteen-year-old William McKinley and his cousin William Osborne watched as volunteers lined up to enlist in a newly formed unit known as the Poland Guards. The two young men felt it was their duty to enlist and were ready to sign up immediately.

Most people expected that the Union forces would win a quick victory that would end the war within a few months. The volunteers at the Poland meeting had enlisted for a three-month tour of duty. When McKinley and his cousin went to sign up at Camp Chase near Columbus, Ohio, they were told that all of the three-month enlistments

had been filled. Anyone who wanted to enlist would have to serve for a period of three years or for the duration of the war. The two young men enlisted in the Twenty-third Ohio Volunteer Infantry. Osborne soon fell ill and was discharged. McKinley, however, served in the Union army for four years.

An Exemplary Soldier

Amazingly, McKinley survived his four years of military service without ever becoming ill or receiving a wound. He proved to be an exemplary soldier who never complained and often displayed bravery under fire.

On September 10, 1861, McKinley got his first taste of action at the Battle of Carnifex Ferry in West Virginia, an encounter that resulted in a Confederate retreat. Recalling the day, McKinley said the battle had given him confidence as a soldier. From then on, "He never went into battle with any fear of being injured—he did not seem to think it possible that any harm could come to him."[1]

In April 1862, the Twenty-third Ohio Infantry joined the Army of the Potomac at Washington, D.C. There, McKinley received his first promotion, to commissary (mess) sergeant. His duties now included supervising the transportation and unloading of supplies and the distribution of food rations. On September 17, 1862, McKinley participated in what became known as one of the most savage battles and the single bloodiest day of the war. On that day at Antietam Creek, near Sharpsburg, Maryland, the Army of the Potomac battled Robert E. Lee's Confederate army. In the midst of the fighting, surrounded by wounded and dying soldiers, McKinley drove a mule team into the thick of the battle to bring hot meat and coffee to the troops on the front line.

Because of his bravery under fire at Antietam, McKinley was promoted to second lieutenant and appointed to the staff of Colonel Rutherford B. Hayes. Impressed by McKinley's heroic deed, Hayes, in a letter home, described the young soldier as "a handsome bright, gallant boy," and "one of the bravest and finest officers in the army."[2]

New Beginnings

In February 1863, McKinley was promoted to first lieutenant. On July 24, 1864, McKinley again displayed exceptional valor at a battle near Kernstown, Virginia. He raced his horse at a gallop under raging enemy fire to give the signal to retreat to a regiment in danger of being surrounded, thereby saving the regiment. The next day he was promoted to captain for his bravery.

By March 1865, the war was drawing to a close. That month, McKinley was awarded the brevet (or honorary) rank of major by President Lincoln. The following month, on April 9, Confederate general Robert E. Lee surrendered to Union general Ulysses S. Grant at Appomattox Court House in Virginia. In the summer of 1865, twenty-two-year-old McKinley returned home

During the Civil War, Second ▶ Lieutenant William McKinley served on the staff of Colonel Rutherford B. Hayes (pictured). Both men would one day be president.

to Ohio. After giving serious thought to plans for the future, he ruled out a career in the army and decided to become a lawyer.

McKinley took a job as a clerk in the law office of Charles Glidden in Youngstown, Ohio. Glidden, impressed with the young man, encouraged him to apply to law school. In the fall of 1866, McKinley entered the Albany Law School in Albany, New York. By March of the following year, McKinley believed he had learned enough to begin working as a lawyer. He returned to Ohio, passed the bar examination, and opened a law office in Canton.

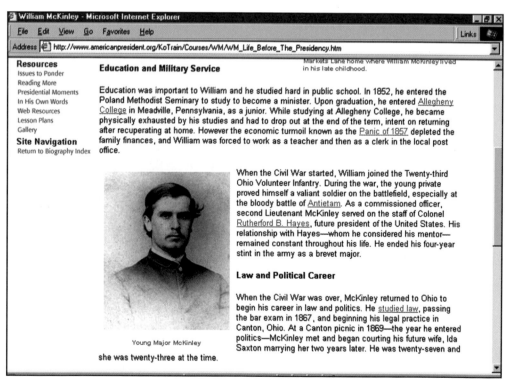

In 1861, when the Civil War began, William McKinley enlisted in the Ohio Volunteer Infantry. In 1862, he took part in one of the war's bloodiest battles—the Battle of Antietam, in Maryland. He was promoted four times before the war's end, at which time he was awarded the honorary rank of brevet major.

Chapter 4

Lawyer and Politician, 1867–1897

Shortly after opening his law office, McKinley became the partner of Judge George W. Belden, an attorney with an established law practice in town. Belden had given McKinley some legal work and was impressed by the skillful manner in which the young lawyer had handled the trial in court. As Belden's partner, McKinley soon became a much-sought-after attorney.

▶ Political Beginnings

In 1868, McKinley became involved in Republican party politics. In fact, his interest in politics was the real reason he had decided to become a lawyer. McKinley was well aware that law was usually the most appropriate route to a political career. Because he was a superb public speaker, McKinley volunteered his time and energy in the 1868 election. He gave campaign speeches on behalf of his former army commander, Rutherford B. Hayes, who was running for governor of Ohio, and Ulysses S. Grant, who was running for president. Both men were elected, and McKinley's contributions were recognized by influential Republicans.

In 1869, Republican party officials encouraged McKinley to run for prosecuting attorney of Stark County, Ohio. He did so and was elected to that office, even though he was a Republican and the county was heavily Democratic.

▶ Marriage

In the summer of 1869, McKinley met the beautiful, young Ida Saxton at a picnic. Ida's father, James Saxton, owned the First National Bank of Canton. At the time, Ida worked as a cashier in the bank. McKinley was attracted to the young woman and found reasons to make frequent visits to the bank. The attraction was mutual, and a courtship soon began. On January 25, 1871, William McKinley and Ida Saxton were married. Among the wedding guests were Governor Rutherford B. Hayes and his wife. Ida's father presented the newlyweds with a house in Canton as a wedding gift.

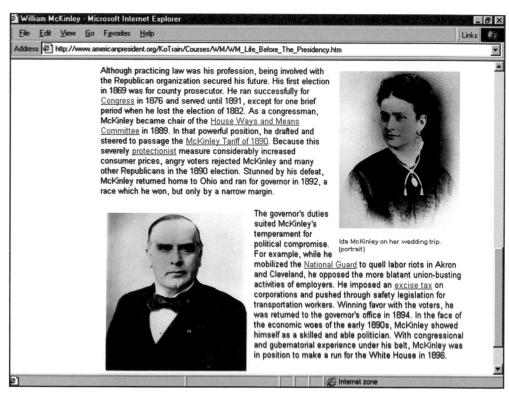

William McKinley - Microsoft Internet Explorer

File　Edit　View　Go　Favorites　Help　　　　Links

Address http://www.americanpresident.org/KoTrain/Courses/WM/WM_Life_Before_The_Presidency.htm

Although practicing law was his profession, being involved with the Republican organization secured his future. His first election in 1869 was for county prosecutor. He ran successfully for Congress in 1876 and served until 1891, except for one brief period when he lost the election of 1882. As a congressman, McKinley became chair of the House Ways and Means Committee in 1889. In that powerful position, he drafted and steered to passage the McKinley Tariff of 1890. Because this severely protectionist measure considerably increased consumer prices, angry voters rejected McKinley and many other Republicans in the 1890 election. Stunned by his defeat, McKinley returned home to Ohio and ran for governor in 1892, a race which he won, but only by a narrow margin.

The governor's duties suited McKinley's temperament for political compromise. For example, while he mobilized the National Guard to quell labor riots in Akron and Cleveland, he opposed the more blatant union-busting activities of employers. He imposed an excise tax on corporations and pushed through safety legislation for transportation workers. Winning favor with the voters, he was returned to the governor's office in 1894. In the face of the economic woes of the early 1890s, McKinley showed himself as a skilled and able politician. With congressional and gubernatorial experience under his belt, McKinley was in position to make a run for the White House in 1896.

Ida McKinley on her wedding trip. (portrait)

Internet zone

▲ William McKinley met Ida Saxton at a picnic in 1869. Less than two years later they were married.

In the 1871 election, McKinley was narrowly defeated while seeking reelection as prosecuting attorney, and he returned to his private law practice. On Christmas Day, their first child, Katherine ("Katie") was born. McKinley's law practice was going well, and he and Ida were very happy. Sadly, their happiness would not last long. In 1873, Ida's mother died, and Ida fell into ill health. Shortly afterward, Ida gave birth to a second child, and the McKinleys named the little girl Ida. But within a few months, the baby died. McKinley and his wife were grief-stricken at the loss of their child. Then in 1876, four-year-old Katie died of typhoid fever. The McKinleys, loving and devoted parents, were devastated. Ida never recovered from those losses.

▶ "The Young Napoléon"

Once again, McKinley became involved in politics, perhaps as a way to help him deal with his grief. In the election of 1876, he ran for the United States Congress and also campaigned for Rutherford B. Hayes, who was running for president. Hayes won the election, and McKinley was elected to Congress to represent Ohio's Eighteenth District. McKinley served as congressman from 1877 to 1883. He was narrowly defeated in the 1882 election, but served again from 1885 to 1891. While in Congress, McKinley became known for his dynamic speeches. Because he seemed to have a magnetic effect on his listeners, people referred to him as "the Young Napoléon."

In 1889, Congressman McKinley became chairman of the powerful House Ways and Means Committee, the committee responsible for raising and allocating the necessary revenues for the government's expenses.

▷ New Tariff Laws

McKinley had always been a firm believer in protective tariffs to protect American businesses from foreign competition. During his first years in Congress, he conducted a thorough study of tariff laws and became an expert on the subject. Many Americans backed his outspoken support for tariffs. They saw tariffs as generally helping to increase the price of foreign goods so that products made in America would be sold at a competitive price. In 1890, McKinley persuaded Congress to pass his new proposed tariff law.

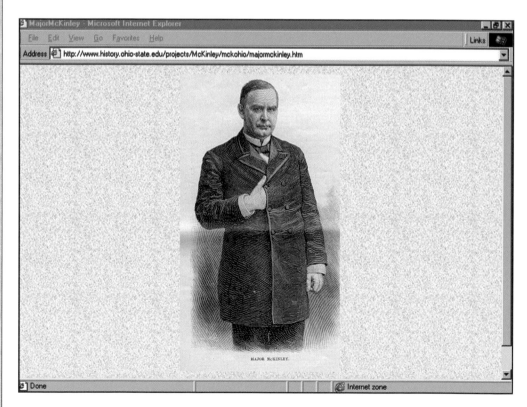

MajorMcKinley - Microsoft Internet Explorer

File Edit View Go Favorites Help   Links

Address http://www.history.ohio-state.edu/projects/McKinley/mckohio/majormckinley.htm

MAJOR McKINLEY.

Done   Internet zone

▲ *McKinley's reputation in Congress as a magnetic speaker earned him the nickname "the Young Napoléon." This engraving casts the Ohio congressman in a pose like that of the French leader.*

On election night, a confident McKinley wrote a newspaper editorial about his tariff in which he claimed, "Protection was never stronger than it is at this hour."[1] On October 1, 1890, President Benjamin Harrison signed the McKinley Tariff into law. The new law taxed four thousand different imported items.

Unfortunately, many Americans who had supported earlier tariffs were no longer in favor of such measures. The lack of foreign competition allowed United States manufacturers to charge higher prices. Although many industrialists still favored tariffs, voters showed their anger by not reelecting McKinley to Congress in the election of 1890. McKinley went back to Ohio. There his friend Mark Hanna, a wealthy businessman, helped get him enough support to be elected governor of the state. McKinley served two terms as Ohio's governor, from 1892 to 1896.

During his first term as governor, McKinley secured safety legislation for Ohio's railroad and factory workers and supported laws allowing workers to form unions and peacefully strike for better working conditions. He also enacted an excise tax on corporations to raise revenue for the state and ease the tax burden on Ohio's citizens. During McKinley's second term, he had to call out the National Guard to put down labor-related disturbances as coal miners and other workers went on strike. However, when he learned that coal-mining families were on the verge of starvation, he sent trainloads of emergency food and supplies to them.

▶ McKinley for President: Election of 1896

McKinley was selected as chairman of the Republican National Convention in 1892, a sign that he was becoming a popular public figure. McKinley received 182 votes for

the presidential nomination, but Benjamin Harrison was renominated. Harrison would later lose the election. In 1896, Mark Hanna helped McKinley win the Republican nomination for president. McKinley's opponent in the election was William Jennings Bryan, the candidate of both the Democratic and Populist parties. The main issue in the election campaign was the nation's money supply. The Republicans favored maintaining a currency based on

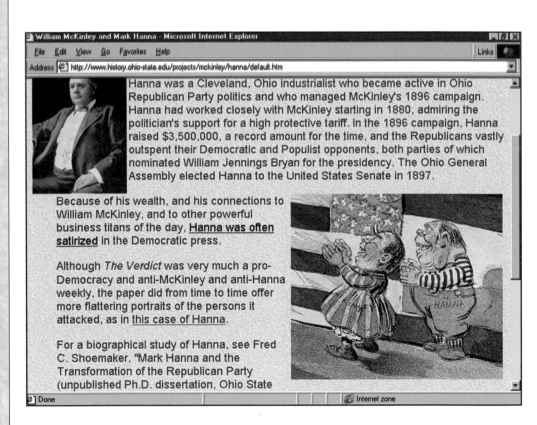

William McKinley and Mark Hanna - Microsoft Internet Explorer

File   Edit   View   Go   Favorites   Help   Links

Address http://www.history.ohio-state.edu/projects/mckinley/hanna/default.htm

Hanna was a Cleveland, Ohio industrialist who became active in Ohio Republican Party politics and who managed McKinley's 1896 campaign. Hanna had worked closely with McKinley starting in 1880, admiring the politician's support for a high protective tariff. In the 1896 campaign, Hanna raised $3,500,000, a record amount for the time, and the Republicans vastly outspent their Democratic and Populist opponents, both parties of which nominated William Jennings Bryan for the presidency. The Ohio General Assembly elected Hanna to the United States Senate in 1897.

Because of his wealth, and his connections to William McKinley, and to other powerful business titans of the day, Hanna was often satirized in the Democratic press.

Although The Verdict was very much a pro-Democracy and anti-McKinley and anti-Hanna weekly, the paper did from time to time offer more flattering portraits of the persons it attacked, as in this case of Hanna.

For a biographical study of Hanna, see Fred C. Shoemaker, "Mark Hanna and the Transformation of the Republican Party (unpublished Ph.D. dissertation, Ohio State

Done   Internet zone

▲ Mark Hanna, a wealthy Ohio industrialist, managed McKinley's 1896 Republican presidential campaign. He had earlier supported McKinley in his gubernatorial races, helping him to become elected the governor of Ohio for two terms. Hanna raised a record amount of money for McKinley's campaigns, and thus became a target (with McKinley) of the Democratic press, as this cartoon shows.

the gold standard. The Democrats called for a "bimetallic" standard of gold and silver.

During the election campaign, presidential hopeful Bryan traveled more than 18,000 miles all around the country to speak to the voters. McKinley, on the other hand, stayed at home in Canton, Ohio. While he sent out representatives to speak on his behalf around the country, McKinley gave speeches from his own front porch. As many as thirty thousand people at a time would crowd into McKinley's yard to hear him speak. McKinley also used the telephone during his campaign, becoming the first presidential candidate to do so for campaign purposes. On election day, McKinley won by a comfortable margin.

Chapter 5

McKinley's First Administration, 1897–1901

On March 4, 1897, in Washington, D.C., William McKinley was inaugurated as America's twenty-fifth president. Garret Hobart became the vice president. In McKinley's inaugural address, he told the cheering crowd, "We want no wars of conquest. We must avoid the temptation of territorial aggression."[1] McKinley sincerely hoped to keep America out of war. His Civil War experience left a lasting reminder of the horrors of war and the human suffering it brought about. However, America was about to enter a new chapter in its growth—a period of intervention and expansion abroad.

▶ Life in the White House

McKinley and his wife quickly settled into the White House and became accustomed to the new surroundings and new routines in their life. Ida McKinley's frequent periods of illness and generally weak physical condition sometimes prevented her from carrying out the duties of a first lady. At such times, the wife of Vice President Hobart would serve instead as a substitute first lady.

McKinley's presidency began on a promising note. He was always a charming and gracious host in the White House. He would listen to requests from members of Congress and respond with the utmost kindness, even when offering a negative response. McKinley still believed in the importance of high tariffs. Congress gave McKinley what he wanted. On July 24, 1897, McKinley signed into law the Dingley Tariff Act, which raised the tax rates on

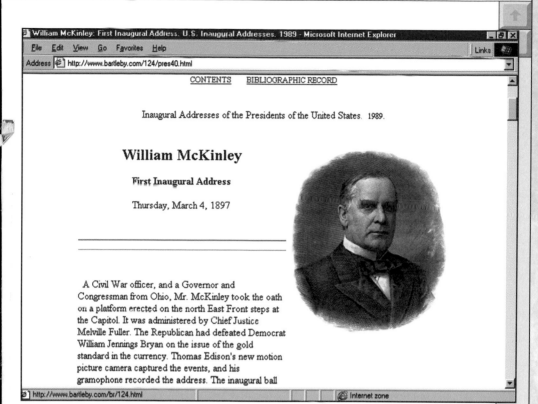

William McKinley: First Inaugural Address. U.S. Inaugural Addresses. 1989 - Microsoft Internet Explorer

File Edit View Go Favorites Help   Links

Address http://www.bartleby.com/124/pres40.html

CONTENTS   BIBLIOGRAPHIC RECORD

Inaugural Addresses of the Presidents of the United States. 1989.

William McKinley

First Inaugural Address

Thursday, March 4, 1897

A Civil War officer, and a Governor and Congressman from Ohio, Mr. McKinley took the oath on a platform erected on the north East Front steps at the Capitol. It was administered by Chief Justice Melville Fuller. The Republican had defeated Democrat William Jennings Bryan on the issue of the gold standard in the currency. Thomas Edison's new motion picture camera captured the events, and his gramophone recorded the address. The inaugural ball

http://www.bartleby.com/br/124.html   Internet zone

In his First Inaugural Address, delivered on March 4, 1897, William McKinley told his audience that he would keep them out of war. His experiences in the Civil War had taught him about the horrors of combat.

imported goods to an average of 52 percent, the highest protective tariff in American history to that time.

An Emerging World Power

Shortly after becoming president, McKinley found that more and more of his time and attention were focused on events beyond the shores of the United States. Americans were becoming increasingly angry at the situation in Cuba. Since 1895, the Cuban people had been engaged in a rebellion against their brutal Spanish rulers. To be sure, terrible deeds were done by those on both sides of the conflict. But lurid

headlines portraying the Spanish as monsters appeared daily in America's newspapers, especially William Randolph Hearst's *New York Journal* and Joseph Pulitzer's *World*.

McKinley urged Spain to reach a peaceful settlement with the Cubans. The Spanish talked about carrying out some reforms in Cuba, but they had no intention of giving up control of the island. While many Americans were caught up in events taking place in Cuba, there were those who focused on the need for the United States to become a world power.

Among those arguing for an expansion of American power were John Fiske, Josiah Strong, and Alfred T. Mahan. Fiske said that it was the destiny of English-speaking people to take over every part of the world not already occupied by an old established civilization. Strong predicted that the Anglo-Saxon race, "the representative . . . of the largest liberty, the purest Christianity, the highest civilization, . . . will spread itself over the earth."[2] Mahan, a naval captain, said that a nation's prosperity depended on its navy and that colonies were indispensable as "resting places" for the fleet.

In early February 1898, the Hearst newspapers acquired a letter written by Enrique Dupuy de Lôme, the Spanish minister to the United States, to the Spanish government. De Lôme mentioned the need for Spain to carry on a propaganda campaign, and he referred to President McKinley as a weak and indecisive political leader. Hearst published the letter under a bold headline, proclaiming it the worst insult to the United States in its history. McKinley was not happy when he learned of the letter.

▶ "Remember the *Maine*"

Then on February 15, the U.S. battleship *Maine* exploded and sank in the harbor at Havana, Cuba, with the loss of 266

▲ *The nearly submerged USS* Maine *is captured in this photograph.*

American sailors. Although there was no evidence that Spain was responsible for the disaster, Americans blamed the Spanish for planting a bomb on the ship. To this day, nobody is sure why the *Maine* blew up, but most naval experts believe the explosion was caused by a malfunction in the ship's own boilers. Still, anti-Spanish hysteria was whipped up by the newspapers, whose headlines cried out for an immediate declaration of war. Americans around the country chanted the slogan "Remember the *Maine*! To hell with Spain!"

By this time, war with Spain was inevitable. Political leaders in Congress demanded that McKinley stop hesitating and ask Congress to authorize a declaration of war. One senator whose patience was at an end threatened, "If he doesn't do something, Congress will exercise the power and declare war in spite of him. He'll get run over and the party with him!"[3] Assistant Secretary of the Navy Theodore

Back Forward Stop Review Home Explore Favorites History

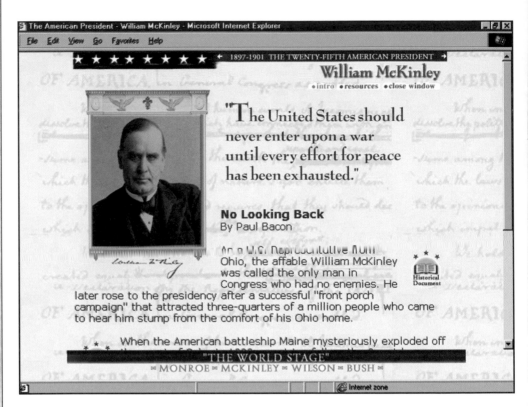

The American President - William McKinley - Microsoft Internet Explorer

File Edit View Go Favorites Help

★ ★ ★ ★ ★ ★ ★ ★ ← 1897-1901 THE TWENTY-FIFTH AMERICAN PRESIDENT →

William McKinley
• intro • resources • close window

"The United States should never enter upon a war until every effort for peace has been exhausted."

No Looking Back
By Paul Bacon

Historical Document

An Ohio Representative from Ohio, the affable William McKinley was called the only man in Congress who had no enemies. He later rose to the presidency after a successful "front porch campaign" that attracted three-quarters of a million people who came to hear him stump from the comfort of his Ohio home.

When the American battleship Maine mysteriously exploded off

"THE WORLD STAGE"
▧ MONROE ▧ MCKINLEY ▧ WILSON ▧ BUSH ▧

Internet zone

▲ *The explosion and sinking of the USS* Maine, *on February 15, 1898, led to a public outcry for war to be declared against Spain—even though there was no evidence that Spain was responsible for the act. Just a little more than a month later, Congress declared war on Spain. McKinley's efforts to avoid war had failed.*

Roosevelt, always outspoken, said that "McKinley has no more backbone than a chocolate eclair."[4] Public pressure for war was building to a fever pitch. On April 11, 1898, McKinley asked Congress for authorization to take action to end the hostilities between Spain and Cuba. Congress granted his request on April 19, and on April 25 declared war on Spain.

On May 1, 1898, Commodore George Dewey, with a fleet of six ships under his command, sailed into Manila Bay in the Philippines, a Spanish possession. The

American fleet destroyed the Spanish fleet. Eight American sailors received minor wounds; 381 Spaniards were either killed or wounded. Suddenly, Americans realized the strategic importance of having a naval base in the Pacific. In June 1897, when McKinley had sent a treaty regarding the annexation of Hawaii to the Senate, ratification was delayed by those who opposed the addition of any new territory. But on July 7, 1898, both houses of Congress ratified the Hawaiian annexation.

Roosevelt's Rough Riders

Meanwhile, the U.S. Fifth Army, under the command of General William Shafter, hastily gathered at Tampa, Florida. The 17,000 troops had little time to drill. Theodore Roosevelt had left his job in the navy and volunteered for the army. He trained with a one thousand-man cavalry regiment that included Western cowboys, frontiersmen, American Indians, African Americans, and an assortment of sportsmen. The regiment became known as "Roosevelt's Rough Riders."

On June 8, 1898, General Shafter's army crowded aboard a fleet of thirty-two transport ships and set sail

During the Spanish-American War, Colonel Theodore Roosevelt led a regiment that became known as "Roosevelt's Rough Riders." Roosevelt had left his job as Assistant Secretary of the Navy to volunteer for the army.

for Cuba. Shafter was a poor planner, and the attempts to load the ships were marked by chaos. Because there were not enough ships, Roosevelt's Rough Riders fought with others to get passage. In the confusion, the Rough Riders had to leave most of their horses behind. When the fleet reached the southern coast of Cuba in late June, there were not enough landing craft. Army horses and mules were lowered overboard to swim ashore. Some panicked and drowned. And there were other problems. The soldiers had been given woolen uniforms suitable for winter weather, not the tropics in summer. And much of the food supply was spoiled.

By now, it had become clear to McKinley that Secretary of War Russell Alger was incompetent, so McKinley decided to direct the war effort himself. The White House became his military headquarters. McKinley hired additional staff and had extra telegraph lines run into the White House. He was now in the position to make all of the important military decisions himself.

On July 1, 1898, Theodore Roosevelt and his Rough Riders, most of them on foot, charged up San Juan Hill, capturing the strategic position overlooking the Cuban city of Santiago. Two days later, United States forces captured the city of Santiago. That same day, Admiral Pascual Cervera, in an attempt to save his ships, ordered the Spanish fleet to sail away from Santiago. Cervera's fleet, consisting of four cruisers and two torpedo boats, did not get far. An American fleet under the command of Commodore Schley intercepted the fleeing Spaniards, and the entire Spanish fleet was destroyed. Within a few days, an American force captured the island of Puerto Rico. A defeated Spain asked for a cease-fire and peace negotiations.

The End of a "Splendid Little War"

By August 1898, the Spanish-American War was over, for all practical purposes. The American ambassador in London, John Hay (who became U.S. secretary of state at the end of September) wrote, "It has been a splendid little war, begun with the highest motives, carried on with magnificent intelligence and spirit, favored by that fortune which loves the brave."[5] Actually, America had been ill-prepared to wage a war in two parts of the world at a moment's notice. The decisive American victory was in

THE NAVAL BATTLE OF SANTIAGO - Microsoft Internet Explorer

File   Edit   View   Go   Favorites   Help   Links

Address http://www.cohums.ohio-state.edu/history/projects/McKinley/Battle_Santiago_Bay.htm

THE NAVAL BATTLE OF SANTIAGO.

A VIVID DESCRIPTION OF THE HISTORIC SEA FIGHT BY CAPTAIN ROBLEY D. EVANS,

COMMANDER OF THE BATTLESHIP IOWA.

Editorial Note: The following account of one of the most remarkable naval battles of the world's history is of intense interest and permanent value, coming as it does not only from an eye-witness, but from a commander of one of the victorious vessels. The story was told to a representative of the Associated Press the day following the battle.

[Scanner's note: The Battle of Santiago Bay occurred on July 3, 1898. The American navy's defeat of the Spanish battle fleet marked the end of centuries-long Spanish power in the western hemisphere. 1,800 Spaniards died in the battle, in contrast to one American death and one American wounded sailor. All of the Spanish ships were beached, either burning or sinking. Two weeks later the Spanish forces defending Santiago surrendered and the Spanish-American war ended. The pictures enclosed here are from the Library of Congress' *American Memory* Collection. For more pictures look in the files of the Detroit Publishing Company.]

"At the time general quarters was sounded, the engine bell rang full speed ahead, and I put the helm to starboard and the Iowa crossed the bows of the Infanta Maria Teresa, the first ship out. As the Spanish admiral swung to the westward the twelve-inch shells from the forward turret of the Iowa seemed to strike him fair in the bow, and the fight was a spectacle.

Internet zone

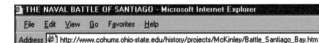

The naval battle of July 3, 1898, in which the American navy defeated the Spanish fleet in Santiago Bay signaled the end of Spain's power in the Western Hemisphere. Two weeks later, Spain asked for a cease-fire.

part due to the Spanish military being more inept and disorganized than the United States forces.

Now that the fighting was over, it was time to bring the troops home. But Secretary of War Alger did not see the necessity of bringing them home quickly. Because of Alger's poor decision, almost all of the soldiers fell ill, and many nearly died from malaria and yellow fever. Theodore Roosevelt's demand for quick action helped the army avoid a disaster. Still, at least 5,000 U.S. soldiers died from disease, whereas only 298 died in combat.

In September 1898, Reverend Teunis Hamlin of Washington's Church of the Covenant offered the following harsh criticism of Alger's job performance: "Whether there have been deliberate crimes against the lives of our soldiers or the blunders of ignorance and incompetence that are as bad as crimes, the public does not yet know. But it does know that in Cuba they were but half clothed, half fed, half sheltered, half doctored."[6] Eventually, Alger was asked to resign, but the resignation did not come until August 1, 1899.

▶ The Treaty of Paris

On December 10, 1898, the United States and Spain signed the Treaty of Paris. Spain formally ceded Puerto Rico, Guam, and the Philippine Islands to the United States. Spain also gave up its claim to Cuba, which would remain under U.S. military occupation until a local government was established in 1902. In fact, Cuba remained a United States protectorate (under U.S. protection and control) until 1934.

Most Americans were thrilled with the outcome of the Spanish-American War. The United States was now a world power, in possession of colonies, capable of competing with the other established players on the world's stage. Ironically, President McKinley, who had appeared weak and hesitant at the beginning of the war, emerged a powerful leader by the war's end. He had not sought territorial conquest. He had not wanted to go to war but had been unable to prevent it. But by taking control of the situation and winning a decisive victory, he forced the United States to become a world power.

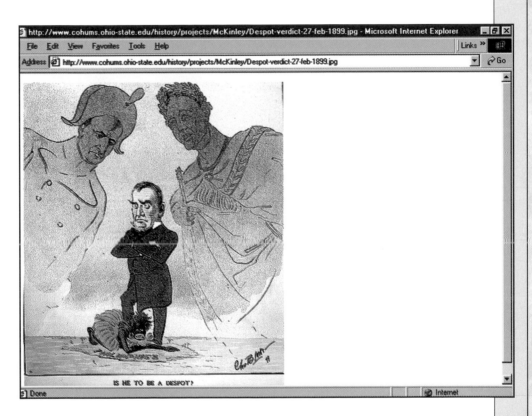

▲ The main issue in the campaign of 1900 was whether the United States should continue its course toward imperialism. The Democrats opposed imperialism, and the Republicans believed it was America's proper course. In this political cartoon, McKinley's policies in the Philippines are being likened to the actions of ruthless rulers of the past.

Conflict in the Philippines

Now that the United States controlled the Philippines, McKinley believed that it was America's duty to occupy all of the islands, educate the Filipino inhabitants, and uplift and Christianize them. Filipino nationalists, who had already been fighting with the Spanish, were not happy to trade one colonizer for another. Emilio Aguinaldo, the leader of the nationalists, said that the United States had promised immediate independence after the Spanish-American War ended. When that did not happen, the nationalists declared independence and the establishment of the Philippine Republic.

McKinley immediately sent military reinforcements to the Philippines to maintain American rule of the islands. Filipino nationalists waged a bitter, bloody struggle against the American forces, resorting to guerrilla tactics in the jungles. The nationalists were finally defeated in 1902, and the United States promised to prepare the Filipinos for eventual self-rule (which would not come about until 1946).

Now that American power extended as far across the Pacific as the Philippines, China beckoned, with its huge markets for American business. In 1899, McKinley authorized Secretary of State John Hay to pursue an "Open Door" policy toward China, in which all nations were to have equal access to trade in China. Britain, France, Germany, Russia, and Japan had already gotten a foothold in China, building railroads, ports, and custom houses. McKinley did not want the United States, as a world power, to be left behind in the scramble to divide up the wealth of China.

The Boxer Uprising

In June 1900, disturbing news reached Washington about massacres occurring in China. A group of Chinese nationalists known as the Boxers wanted to rid China of foreigners, believing they were in China solely to exploit the country's wealth. They were called "Boxers" by English speakers because their combat-preparation techniques resembled boxing. The Boxers started an uprising to get rid of the foreigners. They began by first murdering Christian missionaries and then any Westerners they came into contact with. The Boxers were successful in gaining control of Peking (now known as Beijing), where they killed several foreign diplomats.

As an international force was getting ready to fight the Boxers and drive them from Peking, McKinley decided that America needed to contribute its own troops to the international army in China. Otherwise, when the fighting was over, the Europeans and Japanese would have an even tighter control over the Chinese markets. America might find itself excluded from China, and the Open Door could quickly close. So even though there were few Americans in China who needed protection, and little property belonged to Americans, McKinley sent a force of five thousand United States troops to China. In August 1900,

In 1900, a group of Chinese nationalists who wanted to rid their country of foreign influence, including foreign people, began an uprising. These men became known as "Boxers" because the techniques they practiced to prepare for combat resembled boxing moves.

the American soldiers took part in the fighting at Peking and broke the siege of the city, thus ending the Boxer Uprising. Foreigners were now more deeply entrenched in China than ever.

▶ "Four Years More of the Full Dinner Pail"

In the presidential election of 1900, McKinley once again faced William Jennings Bryan, the Democratic candidate. The main issue in the campaign was the question of whether the United States should be an imperialistic power. Bryan and the Democrats opposed imperialism, condemning the McKinley administration's annexation or control of overseas territories. Bryan demanded immediate independence for the lands acquired at the end of the Spanish-American War. The Republicans, however, believed that not only was imperialism the proper course for America, but that the rest of the world would also benefit from America's "civilizing" influence. Most voters agreed with the Republicans and approved of America's new expansionist role.

Vice President Garret Hobart had died on November 21, 1899, during McKinley's first term as president. So the Republicans chose Theodore Roosevelt, now a popular war hero, as the vice presidential candidate. Roosevelt campaigned strenuously for McKinley, reminding Americans that Republicans had returned the country to prosperity. In campaign stops across America, he repeated the Republican campaign slogan "Four Years More of the Full Dinner Pail." Because the economy was strong and Americans still liked and admired McKinley, he was overwhelmingly reelected to a second term.

Chapter 6 ▶

Second Term and Tragic Death, 1901

On March 4, 1901, William McKinley was inaugurated as president for his second term. Theodore Roosevelt became vice president. In McKinley's inaugural address, he emphasized America's role and responsibilities as a world power. In particular, he spoke about the importance of maintaining friendly relations with Cuba and helping the Cubans develop an effective and democratic government.

▶ An Unexpected Recovery

On April 29, 1901, McKinley, his wife, and several members of his administration began a six-week tour across the nation. They traveled by railroad all the way to the West Coast, stopping in Los Angeles and San Francisco. McKinley's speeches were always warmly received. In San Francisco, Ida McKinley became critically ill and had to be hospitalized. McKinley was so anxious about his wife's condition that he canceled most of the official program. Once again, Americans were reminded of the president's devotion to his wife. Ida's situation had become so grave that she was not expected to live. There were even plans made for a funeral train to Washington, should she die. But Ida made a surprising recovery and was soon well enough to travel. McKinley and his wife then returned to the White House.

▶ The Pan-American Exposition

On September 5, 1901, McKinley gave a speech at the Pan-American Exposition in Buffalo, New York.

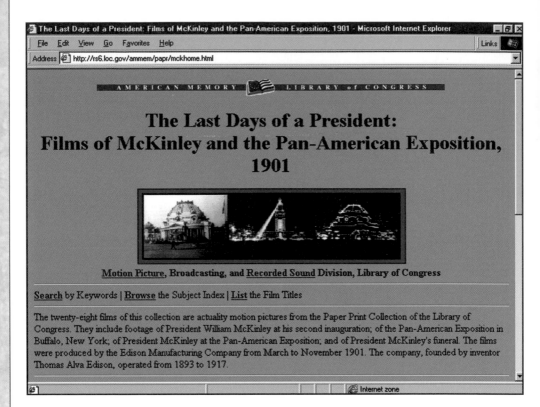

AMERICAN MEMORY · LIBRARY of CONGRESS

The Last Days of a President:
Films of McKinley and the Pan-American Exposition, 1901

Motion Picture, Broadcasting, and Recorded Sound Division, Library of Congress

Search by Keywords | Browse the Subject Index | List the Film Titles

The twenty-eight films of this collection are actuality motion pictures from the Paper Print Collection of the Library of Congress. They include footage of President William McKinley at his second inauguration; of the Pan-American Exposition in Buffalo, New York; of President McKinley at the Pan-American Exposition; and of President McKinley's funeral. The films were produced by the Edison Manufacturing Company from March to November 1901. The company, founded by inventor Thomas Alva Edison, operated from 1893 to 1917.

President William McKinley's speech on September 5, 1901, at the Pan-American Exposition, in Buffalo, New York—his last speech as president—was filmed as a motion picture by the Edison Manufacturing Company. The company was founded by Thomas Edison.

The president, who for many years had taken a strong protectionist stand in favor of high tariffs to protect American industry, now seemed to be changing his position. He spoke persuasively of the primary need for expanding America's markets abroad and the importance of reciprocal trade agreements with other nations. As McKinley said in a speech, "We must not repose in fancied security that we can forever sell everything and buy little or nothing. . . . Isolation is no longer possible or desirable. . . . God and man have linked the nations together. . . . The period of exclusiveness is past."[1]

▶ A Tragic End

The next day, September 6, at four o'clock in the afternoon, McKinley was at the Temple of Music on the fairgrounds of the Pan-American Exposition. As planned, he greeted the public, shaking the hand of one well-wisher after another. One of those waiting in line, however, was most definitely not a well-wisher. At 4:07 P.M., a self-proclaimed anarchist named Leon Czolgosz shot the president, at point-blank range, as McKinley reached out to shake the man's hand. As the doctors were preparing the stricken president for surgery, they heard him softly reciting the Lord's Prayer.

At first, the doctors believed McKinley would recover from his wounds. Several days after he was hospitalized, he was able to sit up and take food and liquid for the first time. The nation breathed a sigh of relief. But a couple of days later, McKinley went into a decline. Doctors realized that the president's pancreas had been partially destroyed, and untreatable gangrene was spreading.

On September 13, 1901, friends and family were gathered at McKinley's bedside. Ida McKinley held her husband's hands as he bade everyone good-bye. He said, "It is God's way. His will, not ours, be done."[2] He smiled at Ida and began to

Upon the assassination of ▶ President William McKinley, Vice President Theodore Roosevelt assumed the office of president, pledging to carry out the policies of the nation's fallen leader.

43

whisper the words of one of his favorite hymns, "Nearer, My God, to Thee." Those were the president's last words. He lapsed into a coma and died in the early hours of September 14. Vice President Theodore Roosevelt assumed the presidency, pledging to carry out McKinley's policies.

On October 29, 1901, an unrepentant Leon Czolgosz went to the electric chair at Auburn State Prison, in New York. Before his execution, he said, "I killed the president because he was the enemy of the people—the good working people. I am not sorry for my crime."[3]

Most everyone else, however, was grief-stricken at the nation's tragic loss. Grover Cleveland, America's twenty-second president, paid tribute to the twenty-fifth president with the following words: "William McKinley has left us a priceless gift in the example of a useful and pure life, in his fidelity to public trusts and in his demonstration of the value of kindly virtues that not only ennoble but lead to success."[4]

Chapter Notes

Chapter 1. "Don't Let Them Hurt Him"

1. Margaret Leech, *In the Days of McKinley* (New York: Harper & Brothers, 1959), p. 595.

2. Ibid., p. 596.

3. Ibid., p. 594.

Chapter 3. Civil War Soldier to Lawyer, 1861–1867

1. Margaret Leech, *In the Days of McKinley* (New York: Harper & Brothers, 1959), p. 6

2. Ibid., p. 7.

Chapter 4. Lawyer and Politician, 1867–1897

1. Margaret Leech, *In the Days of McKinley* (New York: Harper & Brothers, 1959), p. 48.

Chapter 5. McKinley's First Administration, 1897–1901

1. Philip B. Kunhardt, Jr., Philip B. Kunhardt III, and Peter W. Kunhardt, *The American President* (New York: Riverhead Books, 1999), p. 313.

2. Bernard A. Weisberger, *Reaching for Empire: The Life History of the United States, Volume 8: 1890–1901* (New York, Time-Life Books, 1964), p. 129.

3. Richard Shenkman, *Presidential Ambition* (New York, HarperCollins Publishers, 1999), p. 251.

4. William Carl Spielman, *William McKinley: Republican Stalwart* (New York: Exposition, 1954), p. 127, as quoted in William A. DeGregorio, *The Complete Book of U.S. Presidents* (New York: Wings Books, 1997), p. 368.

5. G. J. A. O'Toole, *The Spanish War: An American Epic—1898* (New York: W. W. Norton & Company, 1984), pp. 17–18.

6. Ivan Musicant, *Empire by Default: The Spanish-American War and the Dawn of the American Century* (New York: Henry Holt & Company, 1998), p. 651.

Chapter 6. Second Term and Tragic Death, 1901

1. Margaret Leech, *In the Days of McKinley* (New York: Harper & Brothers, 1959), p. 587.

2. Ibid., p. 601.

3. John Mason Potter, *Plots Against the Presidents* (New York, Astor-Honor, 1968), p. 184, as quoted in William A. DeGregorio, *The Complete Book of U.S. Presidents* (New York: Wings Books, 1997), p. 368.

4. Edward T. Roe, *The Life of William McKinley* (Laird & Lee, 1901), p. 169, as quoted in William A. DeGregorio, *The Complete Book of U.S. Presidents* (New York: Wings Books, 1997), p. 368.

Further Reading

Armstrong, William H. *Major McKinley: William McKinley & the Civil War.* Kent, Ohio.: Kent State University Press, 2000.

Brands, H. W. *The Reckless Decade: America in the 1890s.* New York: St. Martin's Press, 1995.

Collins, David R., ed. *William McKinley: Twenty-Fifth President of the United States.* Ada, Okla.: Garrett Educational Corporation, 1990.

Collins, Mary. *The Spanish-American War.* Danbury, Conn.: Children's Press, 1998.

Gay, Kathlyn, and Martin K. Gay. *Spanish-American War.* Brookfield, Conn.: Twenty-First Century Books, 1995.

Joseph, Paul. *William McKinley.* Minneapolis, Minn.: ABDO Publishing Company, 2000.

Kent, Zachary. *William McKinley: Twenty-Fifth President of the United States.* Danbury, Conn.: Children's Press, 1988.

Steins, Richard. *Harrison, Cleveland, McKinley, & Theodore Roosevelt.* Vero Beach, Fla.: Rourke Corporation, 1996.